x940.1088 Lilly.M

Lilly, Melinda.

Knight /

DATE DUE	
MAR 2 1 2003	JUL 0 5 2006
JUN 1 8 2003	
AUG 5 2003	MAY 2 1 2007
OCT 1 7 2003	
MAY 6 - 2004	FEB 1 8 2008
JUN 3 0 2004	
OCT 2 7 2004	
FEB 0 3 2005	APR 0 5 2008
MAR 0 6 2005	APR 3 0 2008
APR 9 - 2005	
JUN 2 5 2005	
FEB 1 2 2006	

DEMCO, INC. 38-2931

© 2003 Rourke Publishing LLC

All rights reserved. No part of this book may be reproduced or utilized in any form or by any means, electronic or mechanical including photocopying, recording, or by any information storage and retrieval system without permission in writing from the publisher.

www.rourkepublishing.com

For Henry

PICTURE CREDITS: Page 5, MS. Canon. Class. Lat. 274, fol. 1v, courtesy of the Bodleian Library, University of Oxford; Page 6, "The Conquest of Gasgogne by the Armies of Luxembourg, Boulogne, and Artois," from *Fifteen Leaves from Histoire de Charles Martel*, by Pol Fruit and Loyset Liedet (illuminators), illuminated 1467–1472 or 1473, approximately 23 x 19 cm, The J. Paul Getty Museum, Los Angeles; Page 14, "Wachsmut von Kunzingen,"(Cod. Pal. Germ. 848, fol. 160v) from the *Codex Manesse*, courtesy of the University of Heidelberg; Page 17, "Herr Walther von Klingen," (Cod. Pal. Germ. 848, fol. 52r) from the *Codex Manesse*, courtesy of the University of Heidelberg; Page 21, Page detail, "Thomas Moreaux, Marshall of John of Gaunt, Fighting at Ruelles," from *Chroniques (Book 3)*, by Master of the White Inscriptions (illuminator), illuminated about 1480, 48.2 x 35 cm., The J. Paul Getty Museum, Los Angeles; Page 25, "Saint George and the Dragon," from a Book of Hours, by Follower of the Boucicaut Master and Follower of the Egerton Master (illuminators), illuminated about 1410, 19 x 14 cm., The J. Paul Getty Museum, Los Angeles; Page 26, "Simon de Varie Kneeling in Prayer," from *Hours of Simon de Varie*, by Jean Fouquet (illuminator), chief associate of the Bedford Master (illuminator), and Master of Jean Rolin II (illuminator), illuminated in 1455, 11.5 cm. x 8.2 cm, The J. Paul Getty Museum, Los Angeles; Cover illustration and original art pn page 10 by Cheryl Goettemoeller; Original art on pages 9, 13, 18, 22, 29 by Patti Rule.

Cover illustration: A knight in full armor with lance in hand. In the Middle Ages (years 500 to 1500) knights fought for their king or church. As a reward they could own land and maybe even a castle.

Editor: Frank Sloan

Cover design by Nicola Stratford

Library of Congress Cataloging-in-Publication Data

Lilly, Melinda
   Knight / Melinda Lilly
     p. cm. — (People of the middle ages)
   Includes bibliographical references and index.
   Summary: Presents some of the details of the training and life of a knight in the Middle Ages.
   ISBN 1-58952-227-3
     1. Knights and knighthood—Juvenile literature. [1. Knights and knighthood. 2. Middle Ages. 3. Civilization, Medieval.] I. Title

2001056510

CR4513 .L55 2002
940.1'088'355—dc21

Printed in the USA

CG/CG

EVANSTON·PUBLIC
LIBRARY

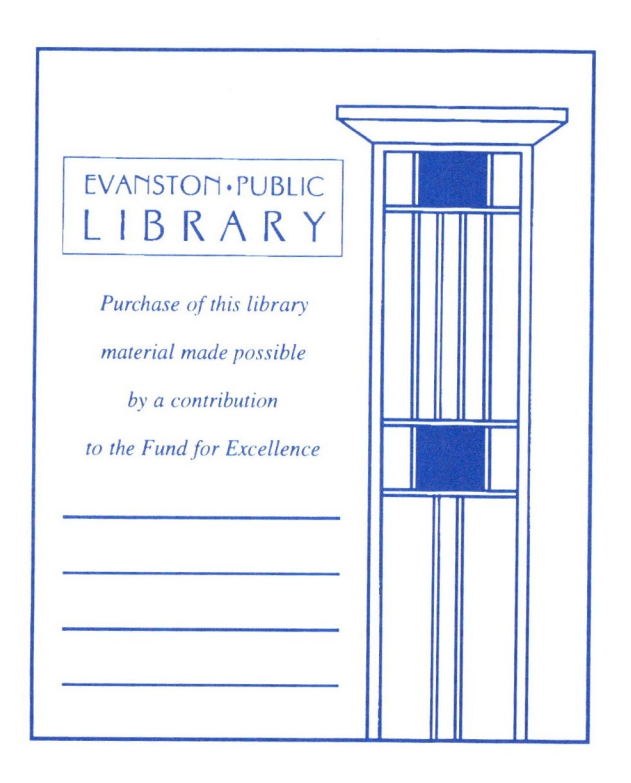

Purchase of this library
material made possible
by a contribution
to the Fund for Excellence

Table of Contents

Stepping into Your Father's Armored Shoes 4
Is the Knighthood for You? 7
A Polite Page 8
Teen Squire 11
Finally, You Become a Knight 12
Your First Tournament 15
Jousting 16
The Brave Butcher 19
Attacking a Castle 20
The Crusades 23
Horse and Sword 24
Who's the Knight Under the Helmet? 27
Longbows and Long Life 28
Dates to Remember 30
Glossary 31
Index 32
Further Reading/Websites to Visit 32

Stepping into Your Father's Armored Shoes

Help Wanted: Boy from good family to protect castle. Must fight on horseback.

Looking for a job? Today you have many choices. It was not that way during the Middle Ages. If you lived in Europe during the years 500 to 1500, you would probably already know what you would do when you grew up. As the eldest son of a knight, some day you would fill your father's armored shoes.

This knight is Alphonso V of Aragon, I of Naples. His picture was painted in a handmade book of the Middle Ages. These books took many years to complete.

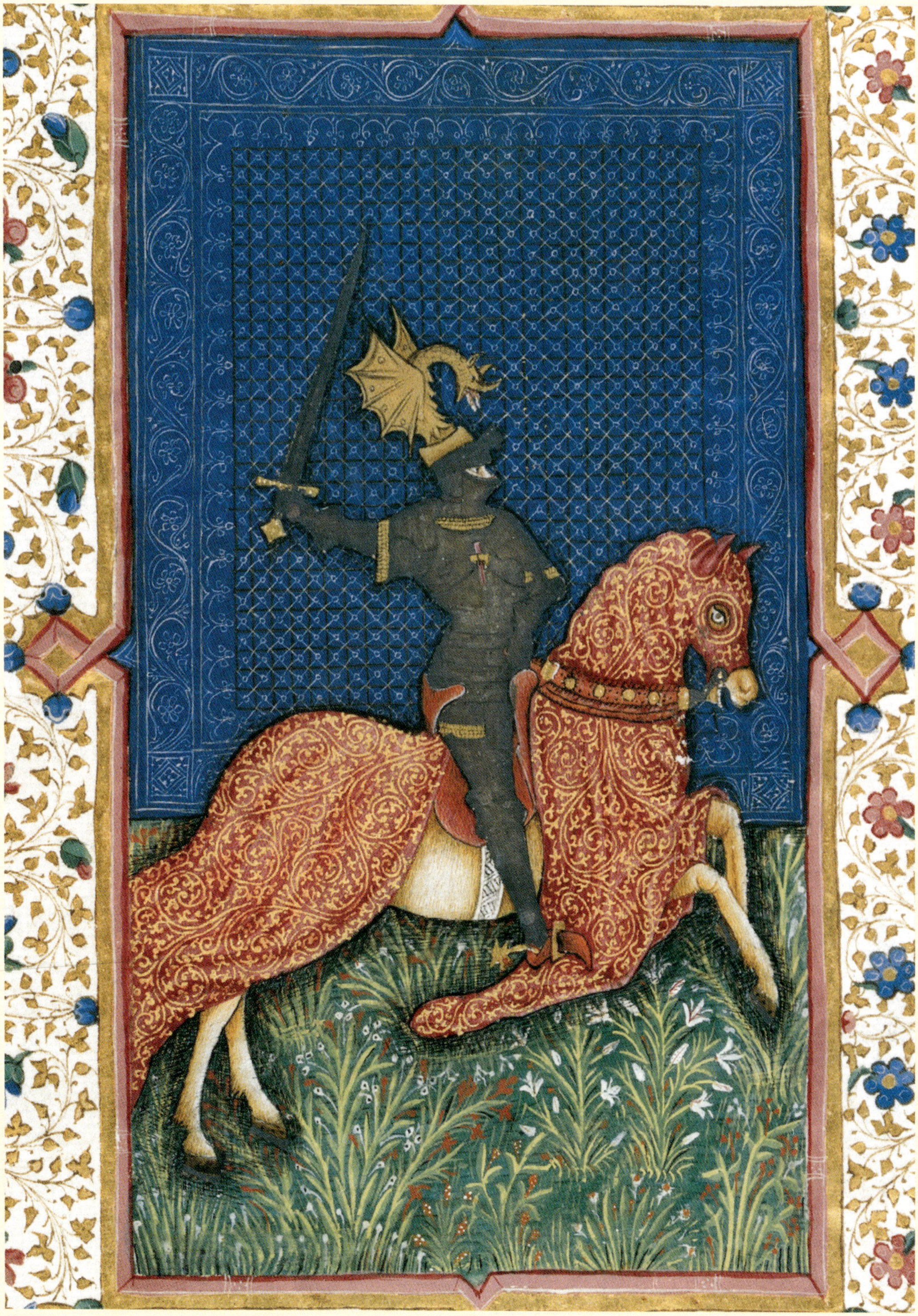

en gasconigne que toutes coururent pillerent et arderent

Coment la terre de gascongne fut conqse par force.

Lancienne histoire racompte que quant le conte guerruier de saint gille quy tres vaillant chevallier estoit eust prinse congie des nobles princes et il sen fut retourne en blesnes lors se misrent a conseil les contes bauduoyn de flandres berenguier de boulongne et gaul-tier dartois ensemble les autres barons pour scavoir coment ilz entreroient en la terre de gascongne affin de trouver leur mortel ennemy Anssere Si conduient puis

Is the Knighthood for You?

Why do you want to be a knight? You might be gone from home for many years, fighting for your king or Church. Your reward is your own land and maybe even a castle.

You can become rich from treasure and other people's land that you win in war. Peasants grow and cook your food. Priests and nuns pray for you. You could even be promised a spot in heaven.

This painting of a battle in France was made for a book in the 1400s.

A Polite Page

Happy eighth birthday, future knight! It is time for you to say **fare wel** (which means farewell) to your family. You will live in a castle as a **page**. Becoming a page is the first step toward knighthood. However, a page's most important duty is to politely serve food.

When not serving, you practice fighting with sword and lance, a long pole with a point at one end. It's more exciting than serving chicken!

A page serves food.

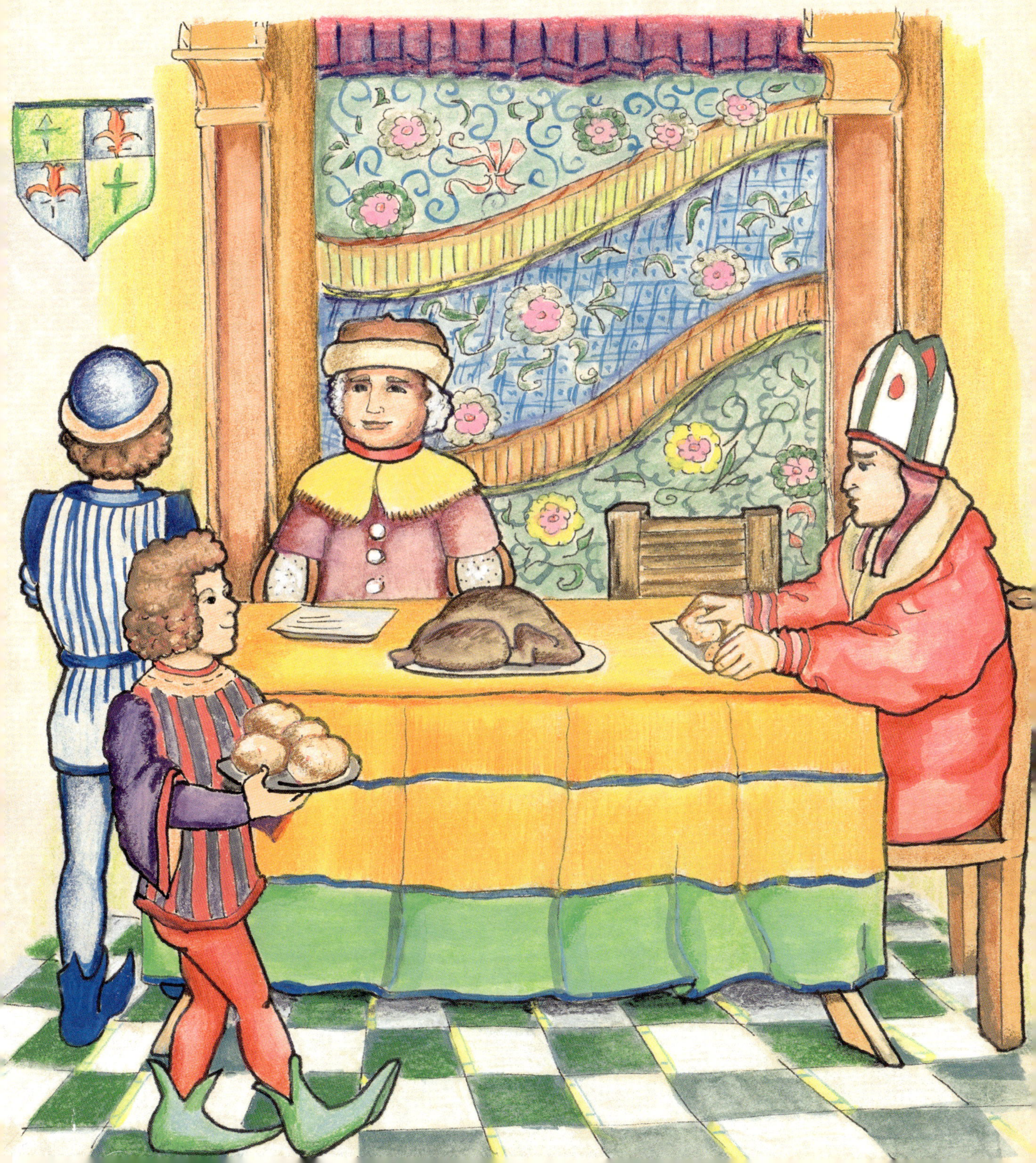

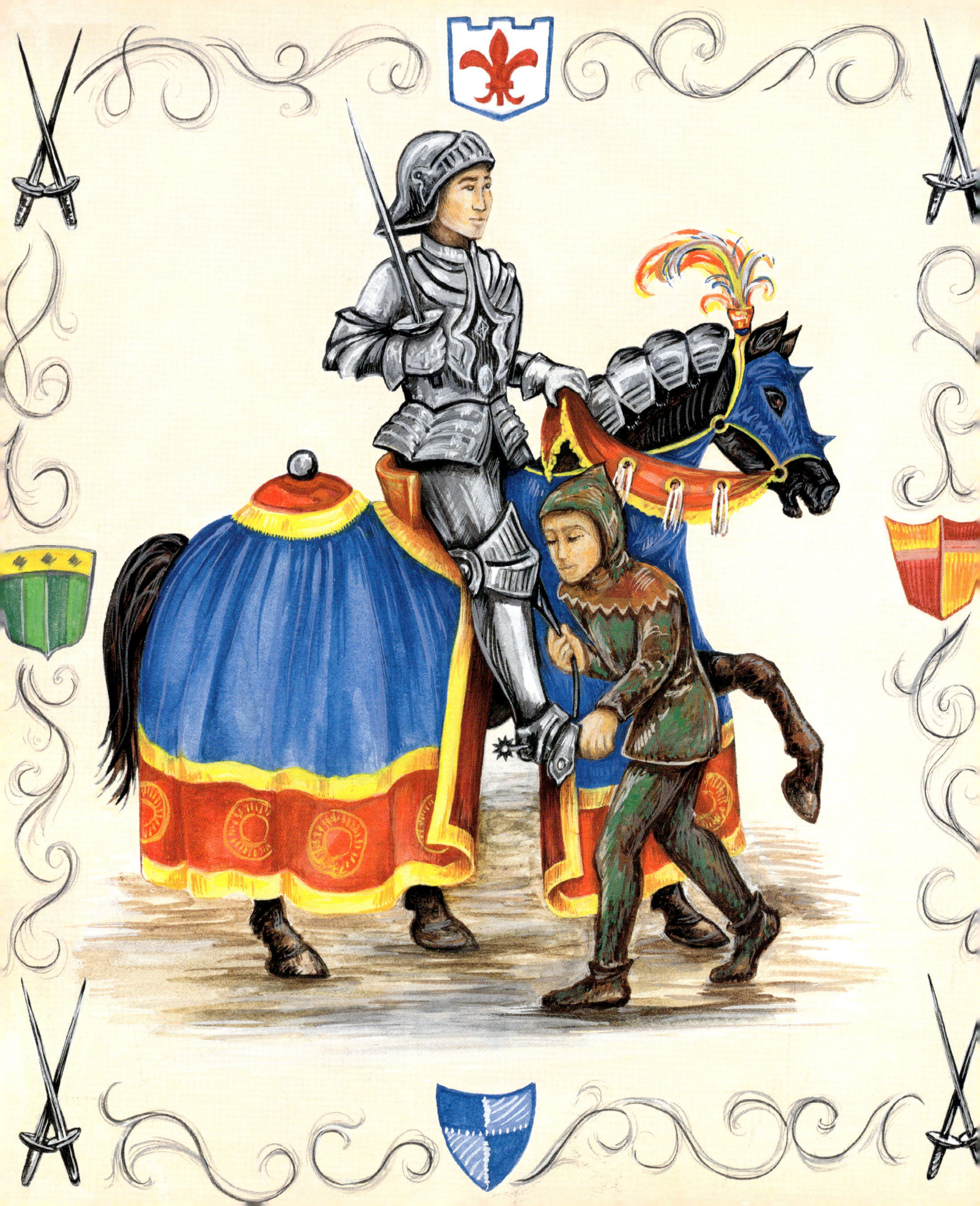

Teen Squire

No more chicken! You have been promoted from page. You are a 14-year-old **squire**. Now you serve a knight. You take care of his horse and armor. You ready him for tournaments, contests where he battles other knights for prizes.

You fight too—in contests for squires and in battle when needed. You and your knight train and travel together. You help him become a great soldier and prepare to become one yourself.

A squire helps a knight get ready for a tournament.

Finally, You Become a Knight

After taking a bath—maybe your only one of the year—you are ready. Knights dress you in gleaming armor and walk with you to church. The priest blesses your sword. You kneel, bow your head, and promise to protect justice, truth, and the Church.

At last, you will be **dubbed**—become a knight. From the 1100s on, most knights are dubbed in a church ceremony. Tap, tap, tap! The sword taps your shoulders. You're now a knight!

A young man becomes a knight by being dubbed.

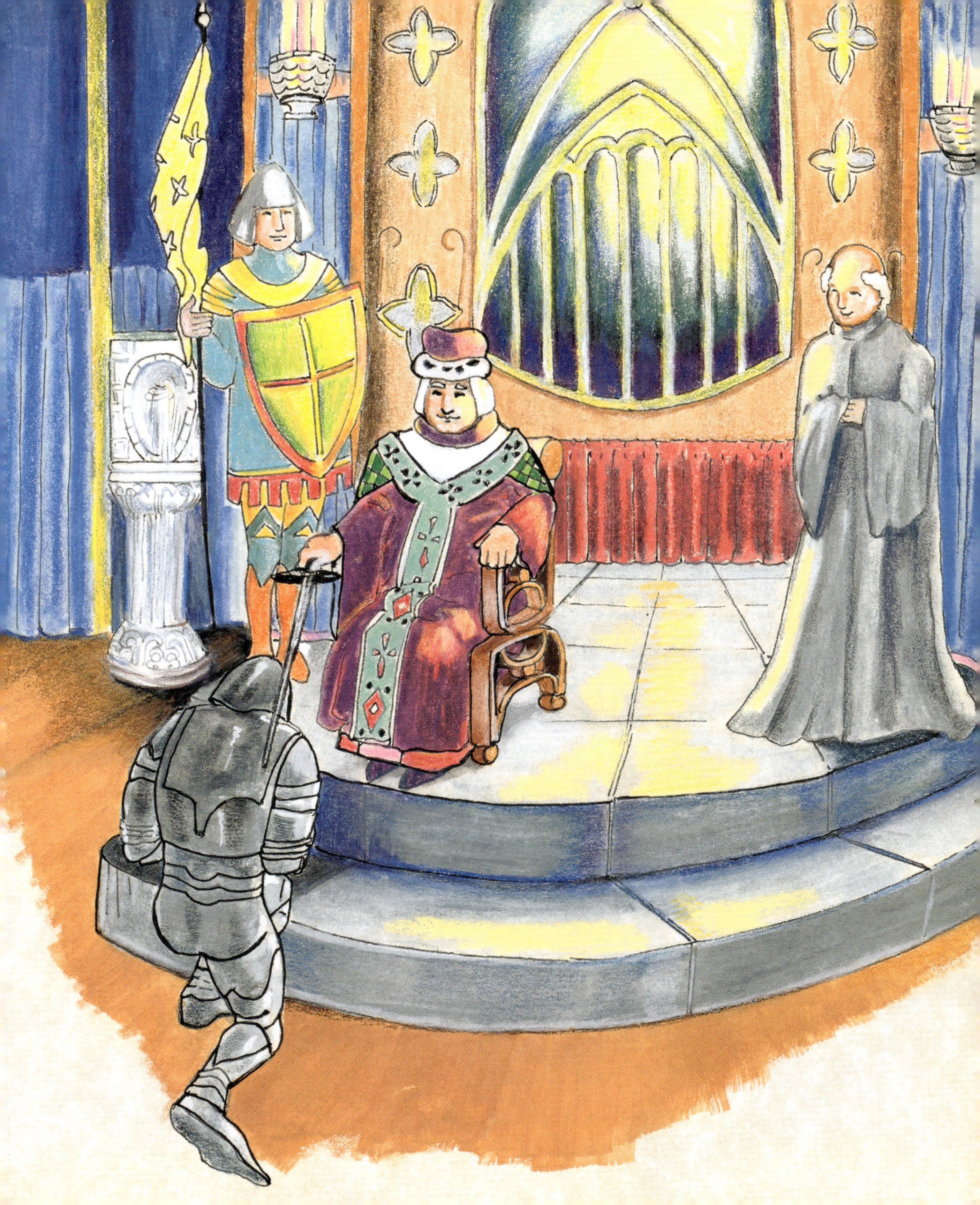

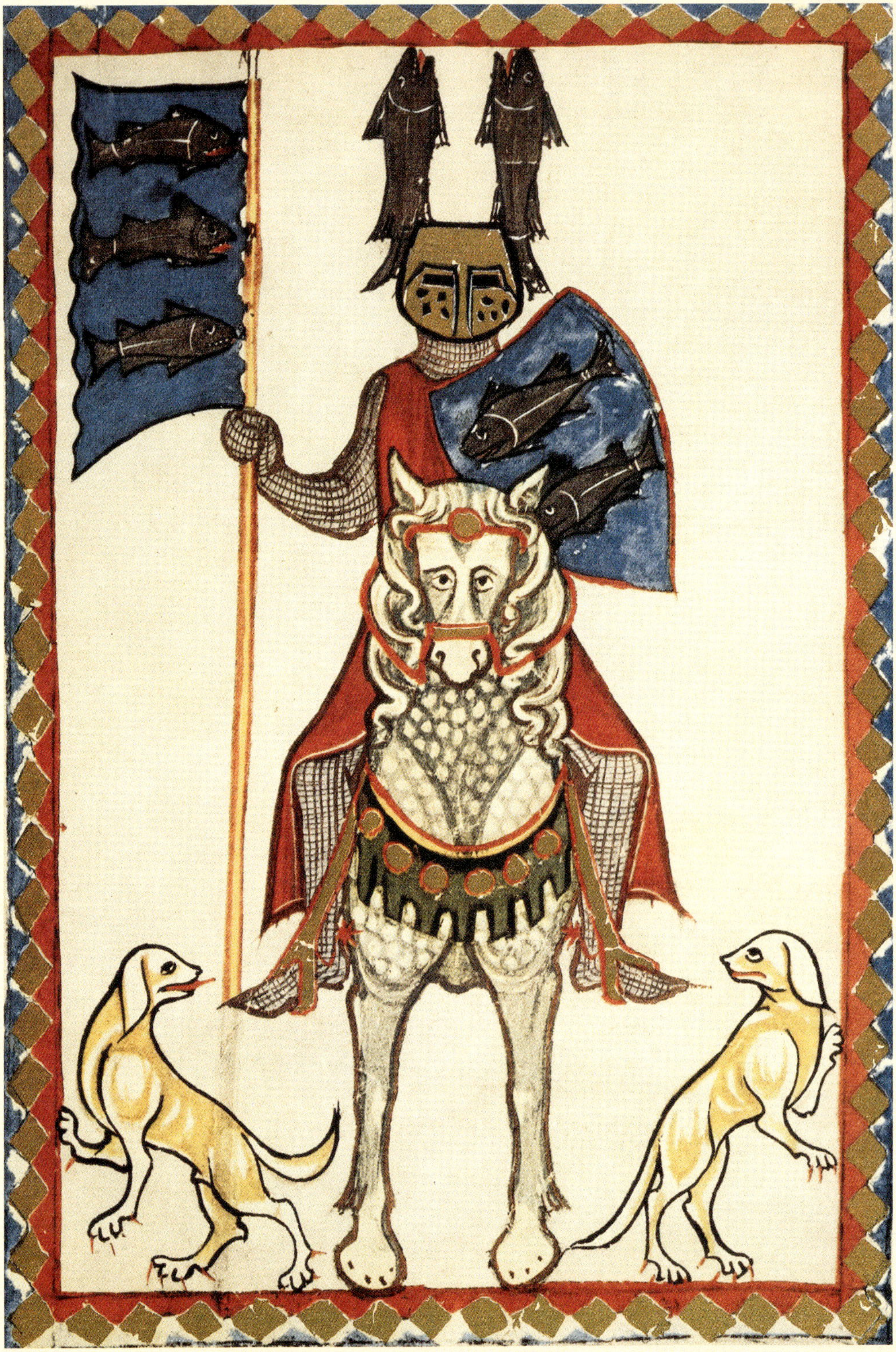

Your First Tournament

You wake up early the next day. It's your first tournament as a knight. Before the 1200s, you would be risking your life. Tournaments had no rules.

Later tournaments are showy sporting events. If you are a Swiss knight, you might wear carved fish or a birdcage—with bird—on top of your helmet! You parade to the tournament grounds. Trumpets blast and performers sing!

A Swiss knight of the 1300s poses with his horse and dogs.

Jousting

Your first event is the **joust**. Blunted lance in hand, you ride to your side of the arena. Listen for the call to joust—charge! Knock the other knight off his horse or make his foot slip out of his stirrup, and you've won!

Later you will fight in the **melee**, when many knights battle at once. That evening, you feast and dance. **Hussa**! What fun!

Walther von Klingen, a knight of the 1300s, wins his joust. This picture is part of a book of the Middle Ages. Its pages were made of very thin sheepskin.

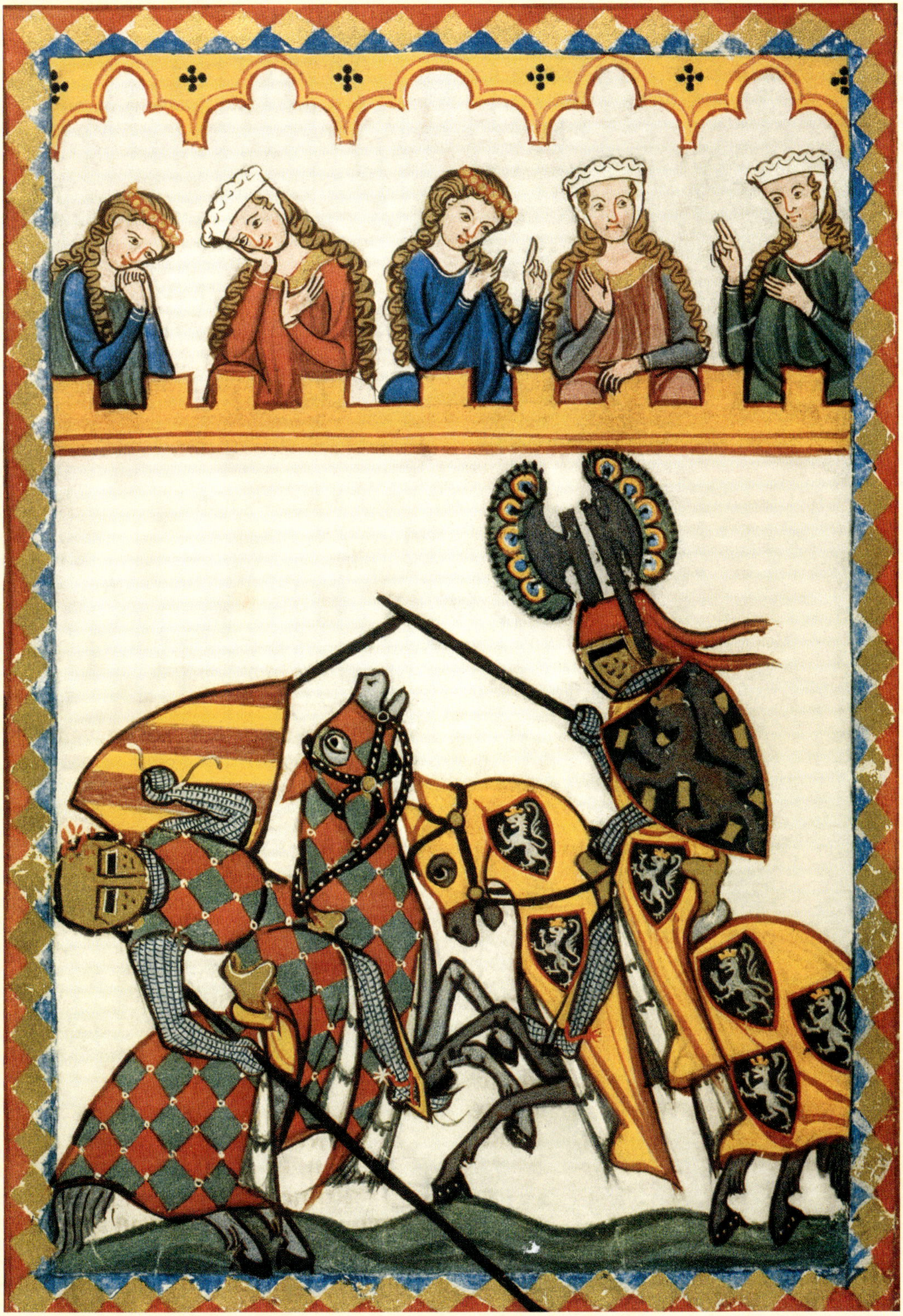

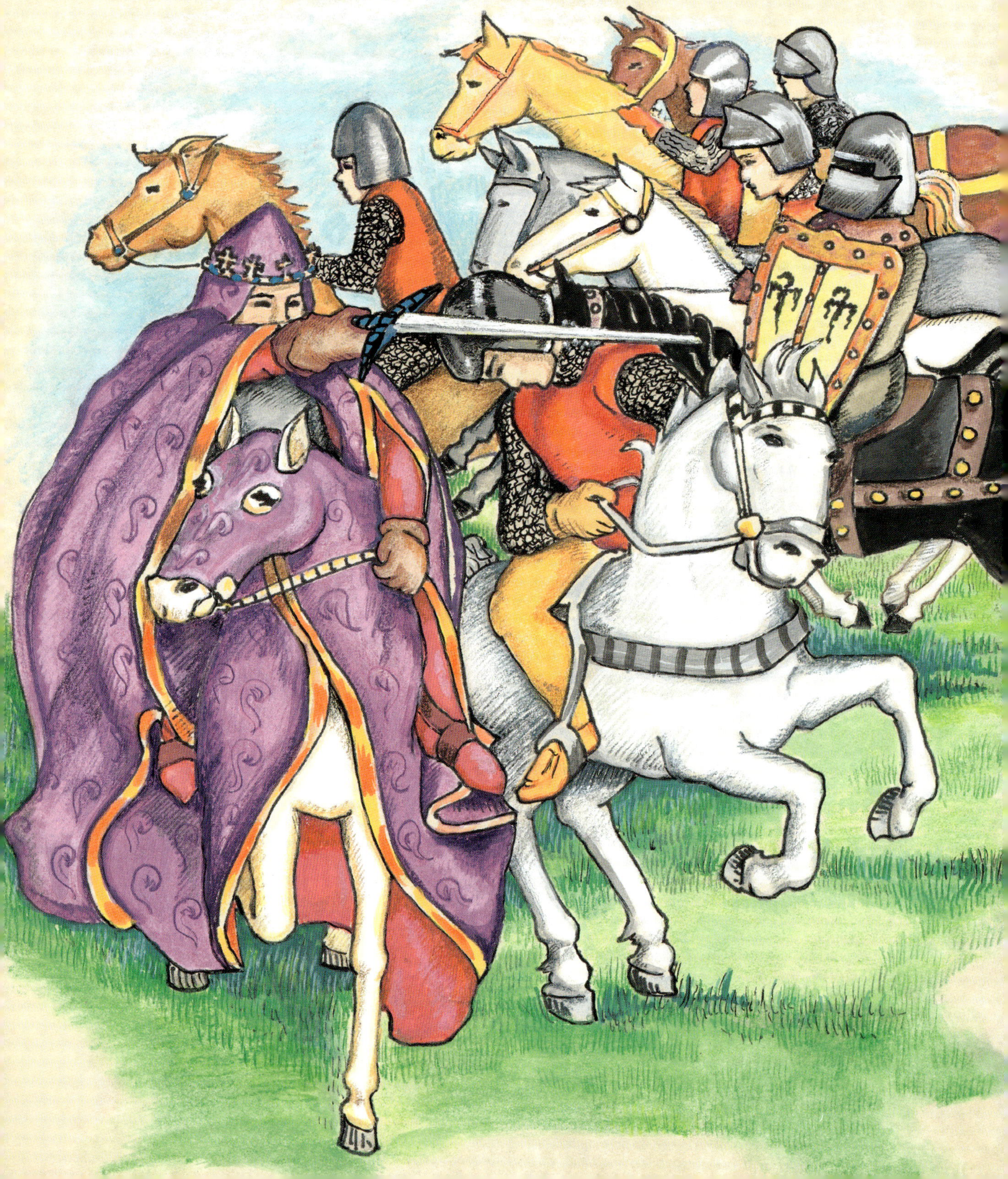

The Brave Butcher

What if you want to be a knight, but are a butcher? There's still hope. In 1303, King Philip of France knighted a butcher for his bravery in battle.

Here's how it happens: You're in the middle of a battle. You swing your butcher's knife and save your king. He gratefully taps you on the shoulders with his sword. You promise to serve him. Ow! He slaps you! Congratulations, you are now his knight!

A king dubs a knight in the middle of a battle.

Attacking a Castle

Your king wants to attack a nearby castle. Along with foot soldiers, bowmen, and other knights, you leave for battle.

Your **archers** shoot at castle guards. Soldiers lay boards across the moat and set ladders against castle walls. You race across the boards and scale the ladders. As you climb, enemies shoot arrows at you. They try to knock over your ladder. They drop rocks and burning balls on your head. . . . Why did you want to become a knight?

Knights of the Middle Ages attack a castle.

Comment messire thommas
moreaulx mareschal du duc de
lancastre print une ville appel
lee ruelles a sept lieues de saint
Jacques seant ou royaume de
castille. Chappe. xxvi.

N ce pendant que le
duc de lancastre z
la duchesse et leurs
enffans et plusieurs
grans seigneurs se logoient en
la ville de saint jacques et che
ualiers et escuiers et compaig
nons uenoient a lauantaige ou

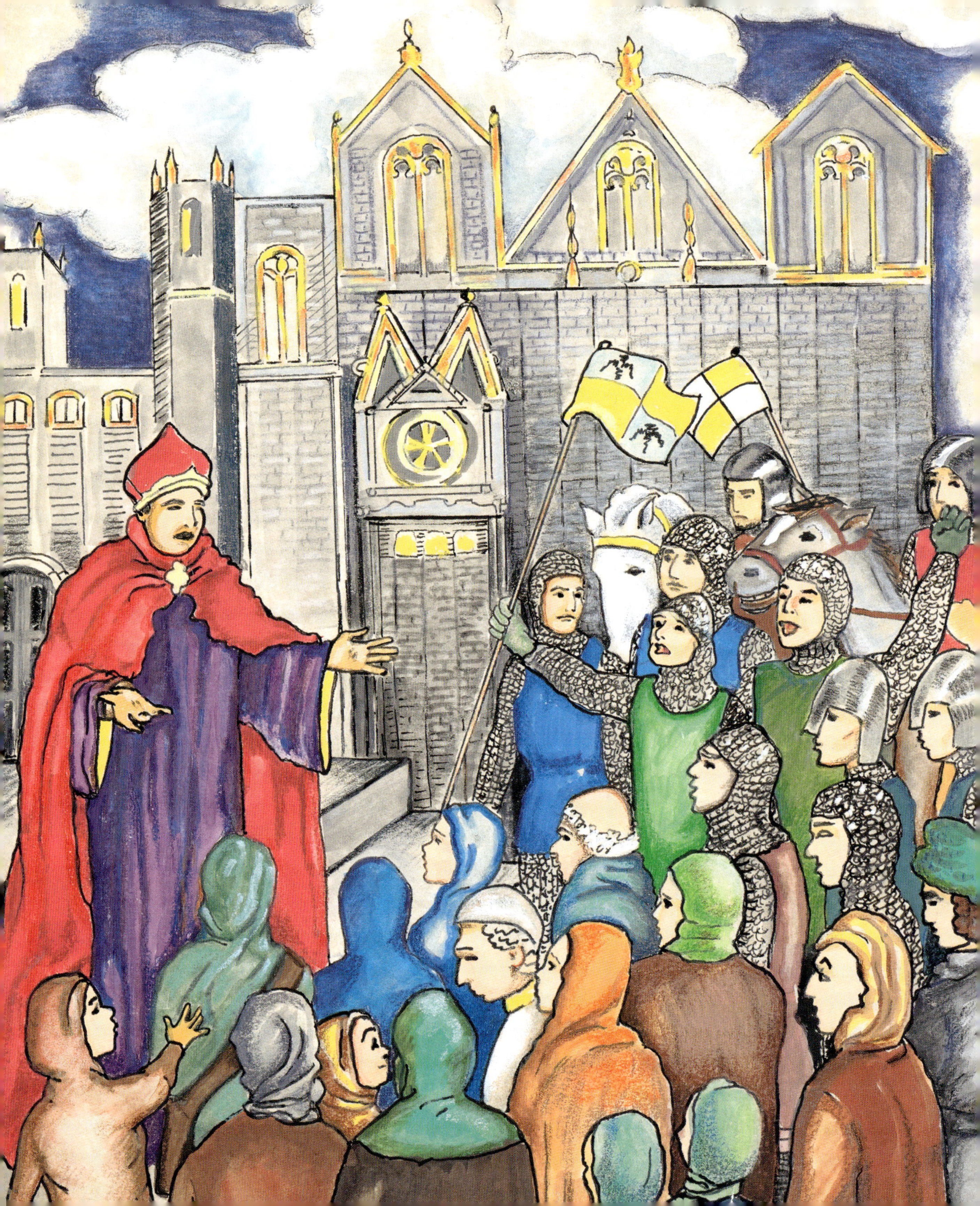

The Crusades

In 1095, religion calls you to battle. The Christian Church wants to control the Holy Lands in the Middle East. This area is sacred to the Muslim, Jewish, and Christian faiths. If you fight, you are promised rewards on earth and in heaven.

These wars, called the **Crusades**, are fought over a period of 200 years. At the end of the brutal wars, the Church still does not control the area.

Pope Urban II, the head of the Church, calls for a Crusade in 1095.

Horse and Sword

Your horse and sword help keep you alive in battle. They also show that you are a knight. Peasants do not fight on horseback and it's against the law for them to carry swords.

Your warhorse is strong and agile. It can charge or sidestep your enemies—even as you swing your mighty sword. The sword weighs two pounds (.9 kilograms) and is 30 inches (76.2 centimeters) long.

A knight on horseback attacks a mythical dragon.

De saint george. antienne.

tleta georgi martiris
rpisti intercede pro nob
ad dominum pro de
uotis famulis. uerset.

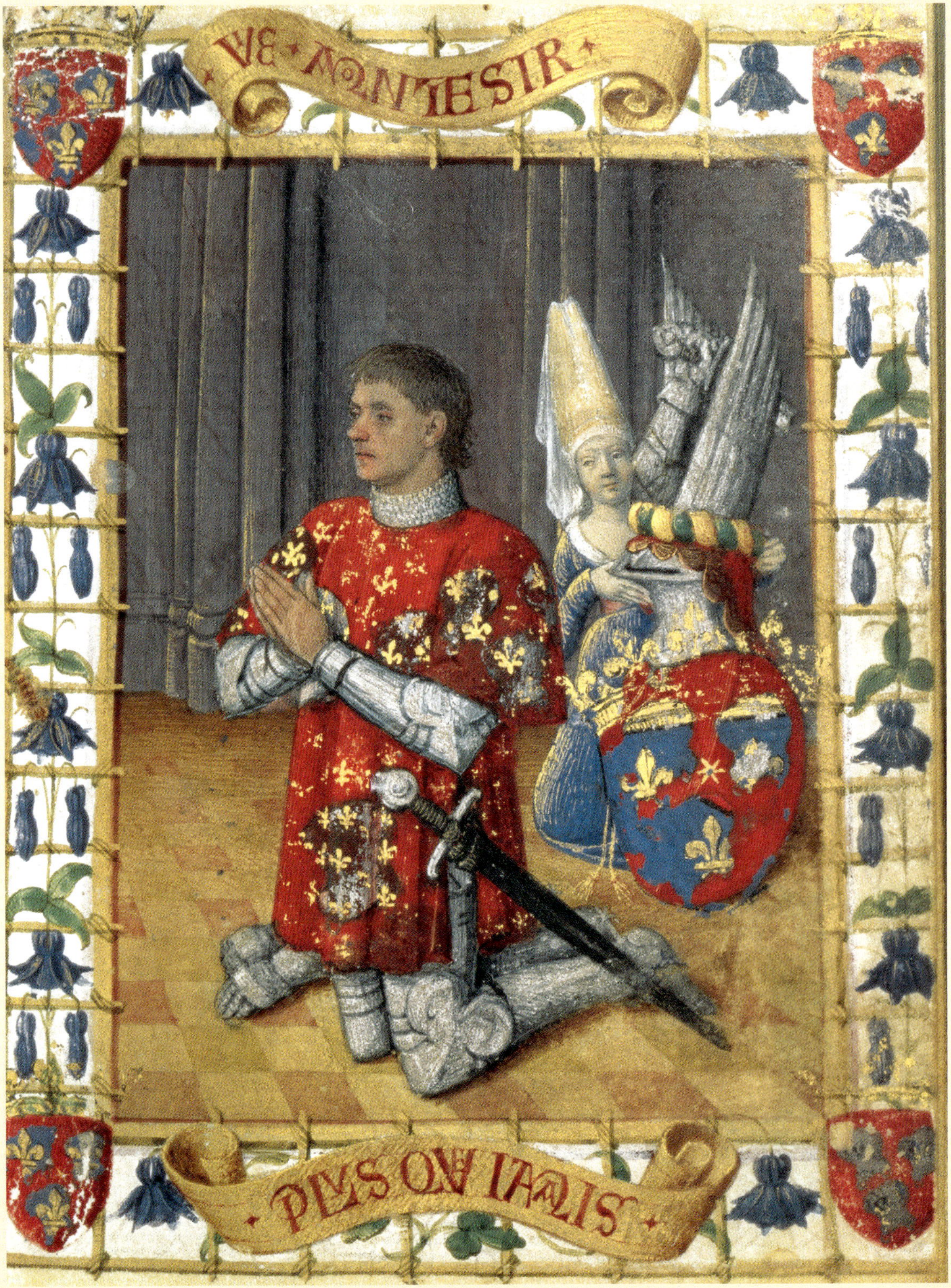

Who's the Knight Under the Helmet?

How can you tell if the knight racing toward you is your friend or enemy? Quick, look at the design on his shield or on the sleeveless coat he wears over his armor. That design is his coat of arms. Only people of his family wear it.

Families choose special colors for their coat of arms. Gold means the sun. Silver is the moon. Red is fire. Blue is sky.

Simon de Varie prays in this picture from 1455. He is surrounded by coats of arms. The designs on his sleeveless coat are those of the French royal family.

Longbows and Long Life

Sick of battles? From the 1300s on, you can pay money instead of fighting. Your king uses the money to hire soldiers. They will fight instead of you.

Soldiers armed with **longbows** are now more important in battle than knights. One hundred longbows shoot a thousand arrows per minute. No one can ride a horse through that! It's time to live the good life at your castle and train a boy to take your place.

This battle shows knights on horseback and soldiers armed with longbows.

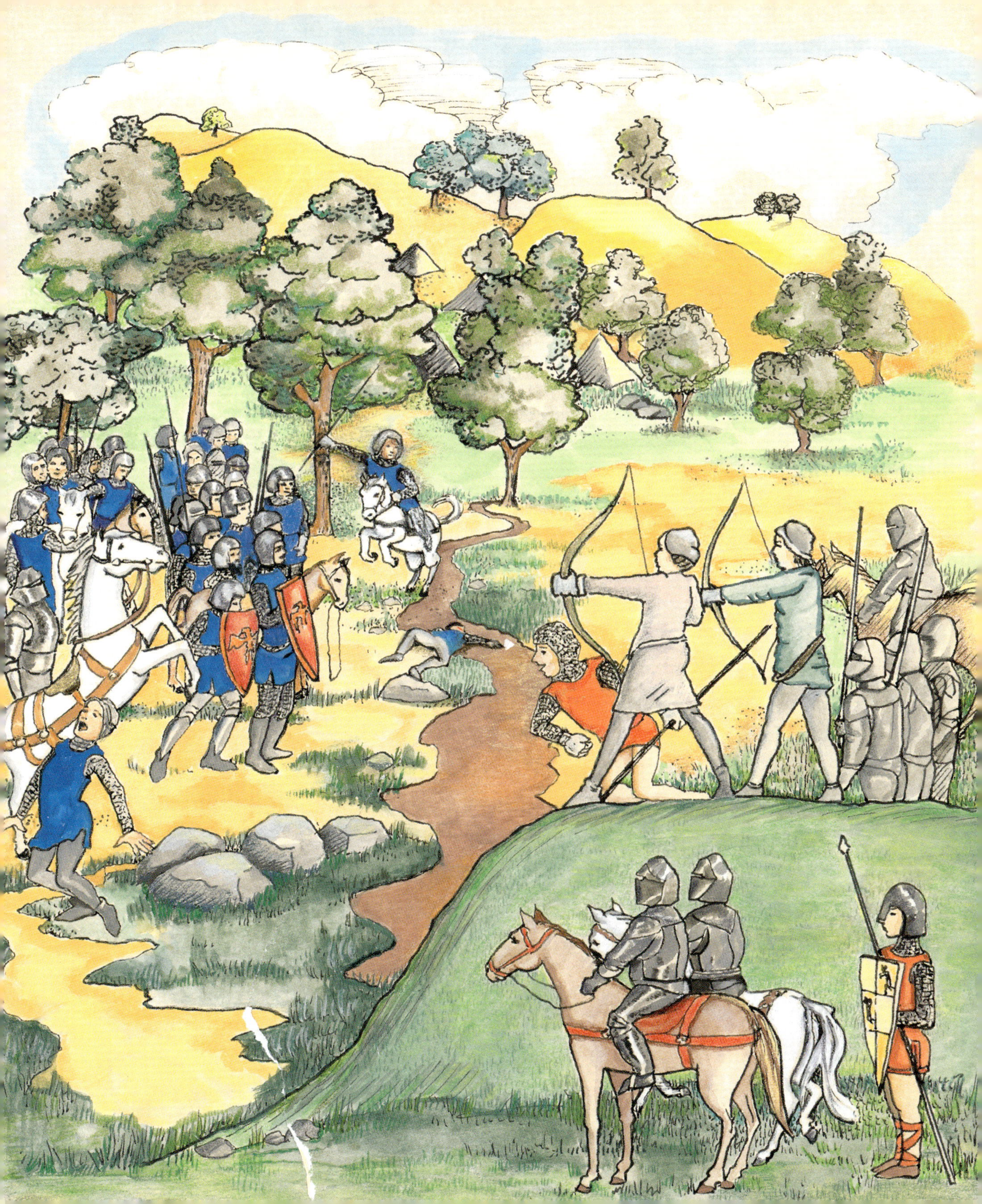

Dates to Remember

476	Last Roman emperor overthrown (Romulus Augustulus)
500	Beginning of the Middle Ages
700s	Stirrups arrive in Europe from China. Men can now fight on horseback without falling off.
1095	Pope Urban II calls for a Crusade to bring Jerusalem under Church control.
1098	The Crusades begin
About 1100	The first tournaments are held
1130	A Church Council (Council of Clermont) condemns tournaments because of the danger.
1291	The last fort of the Crusaders falls to the Arabs and the Crusaders leave the Middle East
1303	King Philip of France knights a butcher
1500	End of the Middle Ages

Glossary

archers (AR churz) — people who shoot with a bow and arrow

Crusades (kroo SAYDS) — wars of the Middle Ages in which Christian soldiers attacked people of other religions

dubbed (DUBD) — to be tapped lightly with a sword in the ceremony that makes a knight

fare wel (fair WEL) — good-bye, as people said and spelled it in the Middle Ages

hussa (huh ZAH) — hooray, as said by people in the Middle Ages

joust (JOUST) — a contest in which two knights try to unhorse each other

longbows (LONG bowz) — large bows used by archers to shoot arrows

melee (MAY lay) — combat in which many people fight

page (PAYJ) — a boy in training to become a knight

squire (SKWIRE) — a young man who serves a knight and hopes to become a knight himself

Index

Crusades 23, 30
dubbed 12
joust 16
King Philip of France 19
longbows 28
melee 16
page 8, 11
squire 11
tournament 11, 15, 30

Further Reading

Gravett, Christopher. *Eyewitness: Knight*. DK Publishing, 2000.
Hart, Avery and Paul Mantell. *Knights and Castles: 50 Hands-on Activities to Experience the Middle Ages.* Econo-Clad Books, 1999.
Rice, Chris; Melanie Rice, Christopher Gravett, and Richard Platt. *Crusades: The Struggle for the Holy Lands*. DK Publishing, 2001.

Websites to Visit

Medieval People
   www.emuseum.mnsu.edu/history/middleages/contents.htm
Created by fourth and fifth grade students
   www.kyrene.k12.az.us/schools/brisas/sunda/ma/mahome.htm
Overview of the Middle Ages
   http://people.clemson.edu/~elizab/medievalgallery.htm

About the Author

Melinda Lilly is the author of several children's books. Some of her past jobs have included editing children's books, teaching pre-school, and working as a reporter for *Time* magazine. She is the author of *Around The World With Food & Spices* also from Rourke.